Touching the Stars

With the butterfly & the monkey

Black and White Edition

Touching the Stars

With the butterfly & the monkey

Black and White Edition

"Do you ever look at the stars?" Asked the monkey.

"Not very often." Replied the butterfly.

"Why not?" Asked the monkey.

"Because they're always there."
Replied the butterfly.

"Just because something's always there, it doesn't mean we should take it for granted." Said the monkey.

"I always feel sad when I look at the stars." Said the monkey.

"Do you feel sad now?" Asked the butterfly.

"A little, yes." Replied the monkey.

"Why?" Asked the butterfly.

"Because whenever I look at the stars, I know I'll never be able. to touch them."
Replied the monkey.

"Have you ever tried to touch them?" Asked the butterfly.

"No, I haven't." Replied the monkey.

"So how do you know you can't touch them, if you've never tried?" Said the butterfly.

"I don't have wings like you."
Said the monkey. "I'm stuck on
the ground."

"But you don't need wings to
fly." Replied the butterfly.

"How will I reach the stars without wings?" Asked the monkey.

"By aiming for them." Replied the butterfly.

"I think I'd be too afraid of falling." Said the monkey.

"As long as you have the courage to get back up, it doesn't matter how many times you fall."
Replied the butterfly.

And so...

they followed the stars.

"It's very dark tonight." Said the monkey, "and I get scared in the dark."

"Even when all seems dark, there is light to be found if we search for it." Replied the butterfly.

"But those clouds look very heavy." Said the monkey. "It might get even darker."

"Once the heavy clouds part, the moon will guide our way." Said the butterfly.

"What happens if they don't?"
Asked the monkey.

"Then we will find another way."
Replied the butterfly.

"You were right," said the monkey, "I can see the moonlight."

"Good things usually happen when you least expect them."
Replied the butterfly.

"Do you think there are predators in those shadows?" Asked the monkey.

"Most likely," replied the butterfly, "but whatever challenges we may face, we will face together."

"I prefer being together, to being alone." Said the monkey.

"So do I." Replied the butterfly.

"Oh look, there's a caterpillar on that leaf," said the monkey, "it's often the small things that make me smile."

"It's not small, if it makes you smile." Replied the butterfly.

"That leaf
came from
an awfully
tall tree."
Said the
monkey.

"Perhaps we could climb towards the stars." Replied the butterfly.

"But you don't have to climb," said the monkey, "you can fly!"

"There's always time to try something new." Replied the butterfly.

And so...

they began to climb.

"Climbing is much harder than I expected it to be." Said the butterfly.

"Why don't you ride on my back?" said the monkey.

"Oh, I wouldn't want to burden you." Replied the butterfly.

"But sharing a burden is often the best way to ease one." Said the monkey.

"Do you think this climb will ever end?" Asked the monkey.

"Everything comes to an end." Replied the butterfly.

"That sounds very sad." Said the monkey.

"It does," replied the butterfly, "but whenever something ends, something new begins."

"I think I see the canopy." Said the monkey.

 "I think I see it too." Replied the butterfly.

"We're very high up," said the monkey, "but still not high enough to touch the stars."

"Not yet." Replied the butterfly.

"I think we should climb back down." Said the butterfly.

"But won't that take us longer to reach the stars?" Asked the monkey.

"It will," said the butterfly, "but the fastest way of doing something, isn't always the best."

And so,

they climbed back down...

"I was really hoping that would work." Said the monkey.

"Don't let go of your hope," replied the butterfly, "it's what gives us a reason to carry on."

"Let's follow this path into the forest," said the butterfly, "perhaps it will lead to something great."

"It could also lead to something scary." Replied the monkey.

"It could," replied the butterfly, "but we shouldn't let fear stop us from moving forward."

"Oh no," said the monkey, "the path ends here... and I don't want to get lost in this forest."

"Then perhaps we should stop following the path and start following our hearts," replied the butterfly, "that way, we'll never get lost."

♡ ♡ ♡

"Look over there," said the butterfly, "I can see a long, green vine... perhaps it leads to the stars."

"But what if it doesn't?" Asked the monkey.

"Then at least we can say we tried," replied the butterfly, "and it's better to have tried and failed, than to never have tried at all."

And so...
they followed their hearts.

"This is a very slippery vine!" Said the monkey, "it's going to take all night to reach the top."

"It doesn't matter how long something takes," replied the butterfly, "so long as you persevere."

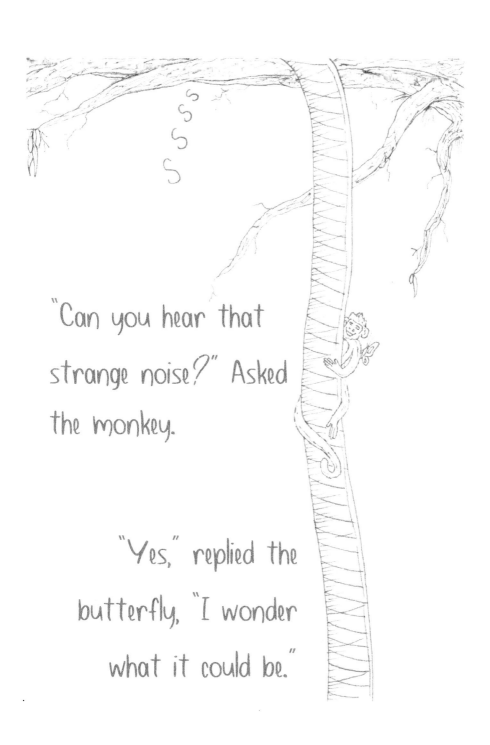

"Can you hear that strange noise?" Asked the monkey.

"Yes," replied the butterfly, "I wonder what it could be."

"I think you'll find it's
me!" Hissed the snake.

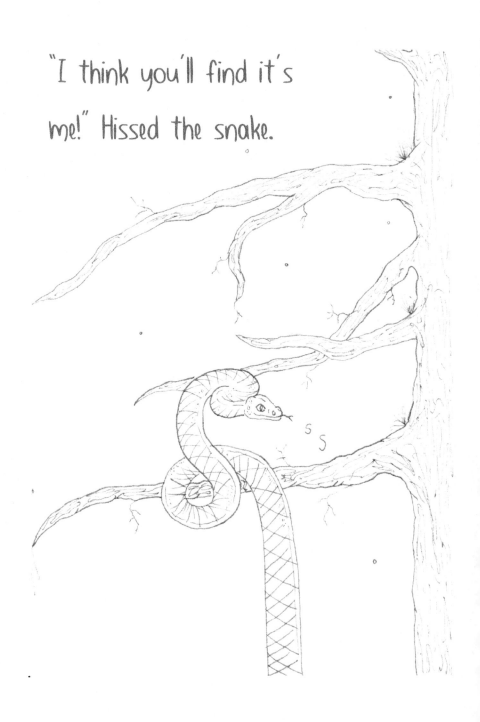

"Oh dear, we're very sorry" said the butterfly "we thought you were a vine."

"It's an easy mistake to make," replied the snake, "but I'm more than happy to assist you."

"That's very kind," said
the monkey, "I thought
you were going to be
angry with us."

"We often assume the worst,"
replied the snake, "but appearances
can be deceiving."

"What brings you this far from the ground?" Asked the snake.

"I've always dreamt of touching the stars," replied the monkey, "but you probably think it's silly."

"Not at all," replied the snake, "Following your dreams is never silly."

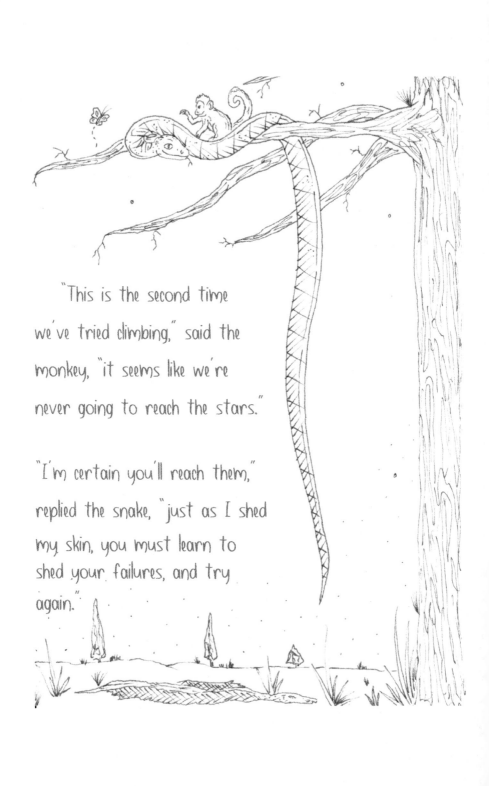

"This is the second time
we've tried climbing," said the
monkey, "it seems like we're
never going to reach the stars."

"I'm certain you'll reach them,"
replied the snake, "just as I shed
my skin, you must learn to
shed your failures, and try
again."

"Thank you for your help," said the butterfly. "I wish I could reward you somehow."

"Being able to help others, is a reward." Replied the snake.

"But there is something you could do for me." Said the snake.

"Of course," replied the butterfly, "what do you need?"

"Would you kindly help me onto that branch," replied the snake, "I'd almost made it up when you started climbing... and it's awful tiring when you're not very strong."

"You helped us, even though you were struggling yourself?" Asked the monkey.

"Of course." Replied the snake.

"Then you are stronger than you think." Said the butterfly.

"How so?" Asked the snake.

"It takes someone very strong to help others with their problems, while they are dealing with problems of their own." Replied the butterfly.

And so...
they helped the snake.

"I hope you find the stars you seek," said the snake, "it was a pleasure meeting you both."

"It was a pleasure meeting you too," said the butterfly, "hard times are often made easier when you're with friends."

SSS

"Look," said the monkey, "there is some delicious fruit in this tree."

"I've never eaten fruit," replied the butterfly, "I wish I was brave enough to try it."

"It's never too late to be who you want to be." Said the monkey.

"I still prefer nectar." Said the butterfly.

"But you only know that, because you stepped outside your comfort zone." Replied the monkey.

"I can see the moonlight again."
Said the monkey

"And I can see the stars."
Replied the butterfly.

"All this climbing is making
me tired." Said the monkey.

"But it is those who endure
hardship without giving up,
who usually succeed." Replied
the butterfly.

"I can't believe how high up we are."
Said the monkey, "I never imagined
we'd come this far."

"Small steps often lead to big
achievements." Replied the butterfly.

"It's wonderful to see the world from up here," said the monkey, "but I still can't quite touch the stars."

"Then perhaps we should focus on the beauty of the moment," replied the butterfly, "that way, we'll always find happiness."

"Look," said the monkey, "there's a big bird flying this way."

"And it flies so effortlessly." Replied the butterfly.

"But first I had to fall," said the bird, "many, many times."

"Is this as high as you can fly?"
Asked the monkey.

"Well, I suppose I could go higher,"
replied the bird, "Why do you
ask?"

"We are trying to reach the stars." Said the monkey.

"Oh, I don't think I could go that high," replied the bird, "but I suppose we are often capable of more than we think."

"Does that mean you'll help us?"
Asked the butterfly.

   "I'll try." Replied the bird.

"Having the will to succeed even
when something seems impossible, is
all we can ask for." Said the
monkey.

And so...

the bird swept them away.

"I've spent so much time looking up," said the monkey, "that I rarely noticed what lay all around me."

"A change of perspective allows you to see the beauty in what you once believed to be ordinary." Replied the bird.

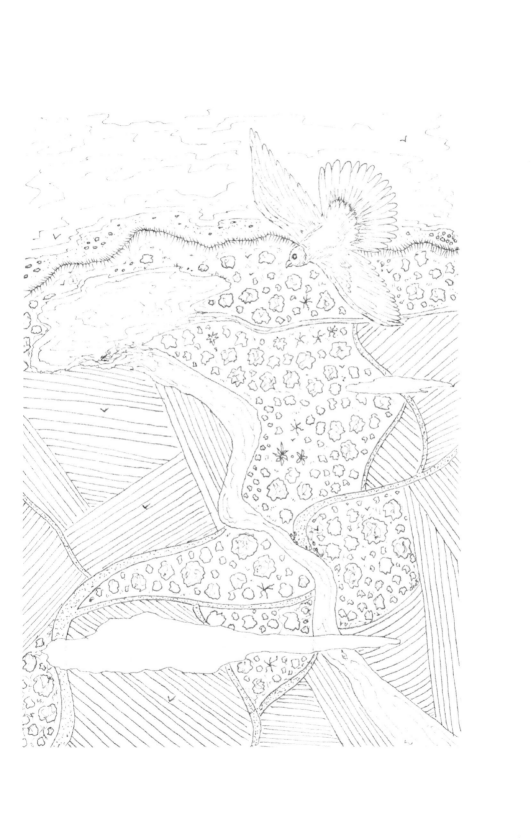

"Look out," said the butterfly, "there's a storm up ahead."

"That looks very dangerous," said the monkey, "I feel scared."

"It's okay to be scared," replied the bird, "but no matter how bad the storm gets... it will always pass."

"I think the skies are clearing,"
said the monkey, "and I don't feel
scared anymore."

"Our emotions come and go, just
like clouds in a stormy sky."
Replied the bird.

"I can't fly much higher." Said the bird. "I'm sorry that I've let you down.

"You haven't let us down," said the butterfly, "your kindness has brought us closer to the stars."

"It was only a small gesture." Replied the bird.

"No act of kindness is ever small." Said the monkey.

"There's a tall mountain over there," said the bird, "I'll put you down on its peak."

"If it's not too much trouble?" Said the butterfly.

"Nothing is ever too much trouble, when it comes to helping a friend." Replied the bird.

And so...
the bird set them down.

"This is a strange mountain" said the monkey, "there's a big hole in it"

"Things are not always as they seem." Replied the butterfly.

"I think it's a volcano."
Said the butterfly.

"But it doesn't look like
one from the outside."
Replied the monkey.

"It's usually what's
inside that matters
most." Said the
butterfly.

A plume of smoke erupts from the volcano, and propels the butterfly and the monkey towards the stars...

"Oh no," said the monkey, "how are we going to stop?"

"A calm mind is the best weapon to use against a challenge," replied the butterfly, "so we must relax, and not panic."

"You see," said the butterfly "it's not too bad now that we've taken a moment to focus."

"But we're still climbing higher." Replied the monkey.

"Yes, we are," said the butterfly, "and that means you can almost touch the stars."

"The air feels thinner up here," said the monkey, "and it's very cold."

"I don't think we can go much higher."
Replied the butterfly,

"That's alright," said the monkey, "I've still achieved more than I ever thought possible."

And then...
they begin to fall.

"We're falling," said the monkey, "just as I feared."

"But we don't have to face
our fears alone." Said the bird.

"You saved us." Said the butterfly.

"How did you know that would work?" Asked the monkey.

"I didn't," said the bird, "but even though we can't control the outcome, we can always control our actions."

"Thank you." Said the monkey and the butterfly.

"You're welcome." Said the bird.

And so...
the bird parted ways with
the butterfly and the
monkey.

"Are you still sad?" Asked the butterfly.

"No, not anymore." Replied the monkey.

"But you never got to touch the stars." Said the butterfly.

"Life doesn't always go as planned," replied the monkey, "...and that's okay."

"Sometimes," said the butterfly, "the unplanned moments are better than the planned ones."

"What shall we do now?" Asked the monkey.

"We could look at the stars." Replied the butterfly.

"I always feel better when I look at the stars."
Said the monkey.

"So do I." Replied the butterfly.

In the night sky, the
stars shine...
and the butterfly and the
monkey continue to
dream...

About the Author

Christopher Stokes was born in an English town called Walsall. He has been fortunate enough to see some of his books become bestsellers in various Amazon categories, and with the constant support of his family, he has written novels, novellas and numerous short stories.
He also turned his passion for art into a plethora of illustrated children's stories, alongside a popular series of colouring books.

You can find him on Facebook at:
Christopher Mark Stokes' World of Colour.

Also Available

Beyond the Horizon

With the cat & the tortoise

Christopher Stokes

Printed in Great Britain
by Amazon

16919426R00061